Break And Retest Trading

A COMPREHENSIVE GUIDE TO BREAK AND RETEST STRATEGIES IN FOREX TRADING

JAMES WILLY

Copyright © 2024 James Willy

All rights reserved.

TABLE OF CONTENT

INTRODUCTION 7

CHAPTER 1 15

Understanding the Principles of Break and Retest Trading 15
    What is break and retest trading? 15
    The Psychology of Price Action 16
    Key Market Principles for Break and Retest 16
    Tools and Requirements for Break and Retest Trading 17

CHAPTER 2 21

Market Structure and Price Action 21
    Understanding Support and Resistance 21
    Importance of Market Structure Levels 22
    How to Determine Valid Trading Levels 23
    Types of Price Action at Key Levels 24
    Volume's Role in Break and Retest Trading 25

CHAPTER 3 29

Anatomy of the Break and Retest Pattern 29
    Parts of a Break and Retest Setup 29
    Different Types of Breakouts 30
    Characteristics of Valid Retest 31

    False Breakouts Versus True Breakouts 32

    Reading Price Action During Retest 34

CHAPTER 4 37

Entry and Exit Strategies 37

    Optimal Entry Points During Retest 37

    Stop Loss Placement Strategies 40

    Taking Profits: Multiple Target Approaches 41

    Position Size and Risk Management 42

    Trading Psychology for Live Trades 43

CHAPTER 5 47

Break and retest under different market conditions 47

    Trading in Trending Markets 47

    Break and Retest in Range-Bounded Markets 48

    Adapting to Different Market Sessions 50

    Impact of Market Volatility 51

    Trading multiple currency pairs 51

CHAPTER 6 55

Advanced Break and Retest Concepts 55

    Complex Break and Retest Patterns 55

    Multiple Timeframe Analysis 56

    Combining with Other Technical Indicators 57

    Advanced Price Action Signals 58

Market Manipulation Awareness 59

CHAPTER 7 63

Trading Psychology and Risk Management 63

    Emotional Control during Breakouts 63

    Managing Fear and Greed. 64

    Position Sizing Strategies 65

    Risk-Reward Optimisation 66

    Creating and Maintaining Trading Discipline 67

CHAPTER 8 71

Common Break and Retest Patterns 71

    Horizontal Support/Resistance Breaks 71

    Trendline Breaks and Retests 72

    Chart Pattern Breakouts 73

    75

    75

    76

    76

    Moving Average Breaks 77

    Channel Breakouts 78

CHAPTER 9 81

Real trading examples and case studies 81

    Successful Trade Analysis 81

Failed Trade Analysis 82

Market Context Examples 83

Various Currency Pair Examples 83

Managing Unexpected Market Events 84

CHAPTER 10 89

Creating Your Break and Retest Trading Plan 89

Creating A Trading Checklist 89

Developing Entry Rules 90

Establishing exit criteria 91

Risk Management Guidelines 91

Performance Tracking and Analysis 92

CHAPTER 11 97

Advanced Strategy Optimisation 97

Fine-Tuning Entry Points 97

Optimising Stop Loss Placement 98

Maximising Profit Targets 99

Adapting to Market Change 100

Strategy Evolution and Refinement 101

CHAPTER 12 105

Common Mistakes and How to Avoid them 105

Early Entry Mistakes 105

Stop Loss Errors 106

Position Sizing Issues 107

Psychology-Based Mistakes 108

Strategy Implementation Errors 109

CONCLUSION 113

Your Journey in Break and Retest Trading 113

Introduction

Throughout my years as a forex trader, I've experimented with a variety of trading methods, ranging from intricate indicators to sophisticated algorithms. Nonetheless, amid all of these approaches, break and retest trading remains a cornerstone of my success. This strong yet frequently misunderstood method has not only influenced my trading career, but has also assisted countless traders in achieving consistency in the forex markets.

I recall my first successful break-and-retest trade on the EUR/USD pair back in 2009. The market had established a firm resistance level at 1.3450, challenged it several times, and eventually broke over with confidence. As a new trader, I waited nervously as the price pulled back to retest this level. Many traders around me panicked, interpreting the downturn as a reversal.

But I remained firm, realising the fundamental truth that previous opposition frequently creates new support. That single trade not only returned 150 pips, but it also strengthened my belief in this trading method.

You are about to go on a journey that will fundamentally alter your understanding of price action and market structure. Break and retest trading is more than just another strategy; it is an essential method of reading and evaluating market behaviour. When you master this strategy, you'll be able to see markets in a new light, identifying previously unknown opportunities.

The essence of break and retest trading is its simplicity. Markets move in predictable ways, breaking through important levels and frequently returning to test them before continuing in their intended direction. It's a pricing and psychology dance in which market participants' cumulative activities produce predictable trading patterns.

Allow me to relate another enlightening moment from my trading journey. During the 2015 Swiss Franc crisis, when the SNB abolished the EUR/CHF peg, many traders lost money using traditional tactics. However, those of us who recognised the break and retest patterns were able to profit from the ensuing moves. Despite the commotion, the market maintained technical levels and produced unambiguous breakout and retest settings.

What makes break and retest trading so effective is its adaptability. You'll learn how this method works for all timeframes and currency pairs. The fundamentals apply whether you're a day trader looking at 15-minute charts or a swing trader analysing daily timeframes. The key is to comprehend market structure and price action dynamics.

In this detailed guide, we will look at every facet of break and retest trading.

From recognising potential breakout levels to managing trades during retests, you'll discover the differences that distinguish successful trades from unsuccessful ones. I'll offer real-world experiences, both successes and failures, because knowing both is critical to your trading progress.

Successful break and retest trading is built on three pillars:

First, study the market structure. You'll learn how to identify critical price levels that are likely to be broken and retested. This is more than just putting lines on charts; it's about knowing why specific levels are important in the market.

Second, analyse the price action. Years of market monitoring have given me a great understanding of price behaviour during breaks and retests. You'll learn to recognise the subtle indications that indicate whether a retest will succeed or fail.

One especially memorable trade was a GBP/USD setup in which the price action during the retest told the entire story - slight rejection wicks and dropping volume indicated an ideal entry time.

Third, risk management. This may seem basic, but I've seen far too many traders with superb analysis skills fail because they couldn't manage their positions correctly. We'll go over position sizing, stop placement, and profit-taking tactics related to break and retest scenarios.

Trading is not just about technical analysis; it is also about psychology. Break and retest patterns frequently elicit significant emotional responses. I recall one USD/JPY trade in which the retest took longer than normal to finish. Many traders abandoned ship, doubting their analysis. Those that understood the psychology behind these patterns and kept their discipline were rewarded with a significant shift in their favour.

As you move through this book, you will see that each chapter builds on the preceding one, resulting in a comprehensive trading framework. We'll progress from fundamental concepts to advanced strategies, while keeping things realistic and relevant to current market situations.

A word of caution: break and retest trading can be quite profitable, but it demands patience and discipline. You'll learn to wait for the right settings instead of pressing trades. In my early days, I lost money by trading every breakout I observed. Now I know better: the best trades frequently result from waiting for obvious setups and valid retests.

The path ahead will need you to reconsider your trading strategies. You'll come to view the market as a flowing river rather than a sequence of random motions.

Each break and retest reveals something about the intentions of market players, and you'll soon be able to read these stories fluently.

Are you prepared to learn one of the most dependable trading tactics in the forex market? Let's embark on this adventure together, experiencing the interesting world of break and retest trading.

Chapter 1

Understanding the Principles of Break and Retest Trading

What is break and retest trading?

The underlying market behaviour of price breaking through major levels and returning to test them is central to the break and retest trading principle. I've seen this trend dozens of times across multiple currency combinations. When price breaks through a support or resistance level, it typically returns to test it from the other side. This retest confirms the level's role reversal.

The Psychology of Price Action

All movements in forex trading are driven by market psychology. Major financial institutions, retail traders, and algorithmic systems all collaborate to generate patterns that we may identify and trade. Throughout my trading career, I've seen how fear and greed materialise in break and retest patterns. When price breaks a level, some traders follow the rise, while others wait for a pullback. This psychological fight results in the retest phenomenon.

Key Market Principles for Break and Retest

Several fundamental ideas underpin break and retest trading reliability. First, consider the principle of role reversal: past support becomes resistance, and vice versa. Second, the market memory principle states that prices tend to react to levels where significant trading activity has occurred in the past. Third, consider the principle of price momentum: significant breaks frequently result in persistent moves following successful retests. I've built my trading career on these fundamental ideas, having witnessed them play out repeatedly in the FX market.

Tools and Requirements for Break and Retest Trading

To successfully trade breaks and retests, you'll need precise tools and conditions. A clean price chart with clear price activity is essential. While indicators can be useful, they should not take precedence over raw price action. Your trading platform should deliver accurate data and quick execution. After years of trading, I discovered that keeping my toolkit simple - support/resistance levels, trendlines, and volume analysis - produces the best outcomes.

The Function of Market Structure in Break and Retest Patterns

Market structure provides the framework for the development of break and retest patterns. During my USD/JPY trades, I learnt how to identify the market structure hierarchy, which ranges from large swing highs and lows to tiny support and resistance levels. Understanding market structure allows you to distinguish between large breaks that are likely to yield consistent retests and tiny breaks that may fail.

Every aspect of the market structure is important. Swinging highs and lows provide a bigger framework. Trending markets provide breaks and retests that are consistent with the trend. Ranging markets generate opportunities at the range boundaries. Understanding how these structural variables interact with price action is essential.

I trade solely on market structure research mixed with break and retest patterns. This strategy has proven reliable in a variety of market scenarios. Focussing on strong market structure levels can help you identify and trade break and retest patterns.

The most successful break and retest trades take place where many structural elements intersect. When price breaks through a significant level that is consistent with the entire market structure, the likelihood of a successful trade rises dramatically. These high-probability setups provide the foundation for consistent trading performance.

I've learnt through years of trading that following market structure differentiates profitable break and retest trades from losses.

Each market structure level provides a story about recent trading activity, and understanding these stories allows for more accurate predictions of future price behaviour.

Chapter 2

Market Structure and Price Action

Understanding Support and Resistance.

Support and resistance are the foundation of market structure analysis in forex trading. Through my significant trading expertise, I've learnt that these levels are more than just lines on a chart; they indicate zones where major buying and selling decisions are made. Support levels are areas where buying pressure outweighs selling pressure, and resistance levels are zones where sellers outnumber buyers.

Working with the EUR/USD pair taught me that the most powerful support and resistance levels frequently emerge at psychologically significant prices, such as 1.1000 or 1.1500. These levels are particularly significant since major institutional traders and automated systems frequently place orders around these figures. You'll see that price frequently respects these levels, allowing for break and retest trades.

Importance of Market Structure Levels

Market structure levels provide the foundation for all price movements. In my trading, I've recognised three primary structural levels: major, intermediate, and minor. Major levels usually occur at significant market turning events, and they produce the most consistent break and retest patterns.

Intermediate levels form during trending advances, whilst minor levels arise during short-term price variations.

The strength of a market structure level is strongly related to the time frame in which it arises and the quantity of price interaction it has received. During my GBP/USD trades, levels with multiple touches over several weeks or months proved more trustworthy than those produced over shorter time periods.

How to Determine Valid Trading Levels

Identifying valid trading levels necessitates a thorough understanding of price behaviour. I seek for areas where the price has reversed numerous times, resulting in clear rejection wicks on the candlestick. The more times a level is tested, the more significant it is. Valid levels frequently coincide with past swing highs or lows, underlining their importance.

When tested at strong market structure levels, there is usually unequivocal price rejection. These rejections appear as long wicks on candlesticks, indicating that buyers or sellers acted strongly at these points. Through years of study, I've discovered that the most trustworthy levels frequently exhibit this type of price movement.

Types of Price Action at Key Levels

Price behaves differently as it approaches crucial structural levels. During my USD/JPY trading sessions, I noticed numerous recurrent patterns. Price can sometimes approach a level slowly and with decreasing momentum, indicating a likely rejection. Sometimes it pushes aggressively towards the level, indicating a potential break.

The candlestick patterns formed at these levels provide information regarding market sentiment.

Large-bodied candles indicate strong conviction from either buyers or sellers. Small bodies with lengthy wicks suggest indecision and possible reversal. These patterns are especially significant when they occur at established market structure levels.

Volume's Role in Break and Retest Trading

Volume provides critical confirmation for break and retest configurations. In my experience trading the AUD/USD, true breakouts are usually accompanied by increasing volume, whereas false breaks are frequently accompanied by low volume. During retests, dropping volume frequently signals that the pullback is losing steam, implying that the breakout trend may continue.

High volume during a break indicates active market participation and raises the opportunity of a successful trade.

I pay close attention to volume patterns throughout both the break and retest phases. A legitimate break should have above-average volume, although retests frequently occur on dropping volume.

The most consistent setups arise when price action and volume coincide at significant market structure levels. For example, a break of key resistance on high volume, followed by a retest on lower volume, frequently results in good trading opportunities. These patterns have frequently demonstrated themselves in my personal trading.

Understanding market structure and price movement requires time and experience. During my years in the forex market, I've learnt to read these patterns like a language. Each level depicts the story of where significant players place their orders. When you comprehend this language, you'll be able to identify high-probability trading opportunity more readily.

The secret to success is patience and discipline. Not all levels will produce a tradeable break and retest pattern. Some levels may be checked several times before a valid break occurs. Others may break cleanly, but fail to give a retest. Your goal as a trader is to wait for setups that correspond to your trading rules and risk parameters.

Remember that market structure is dynamic, not static. Levels that were significant in the past may lose importance over time, while new levels emerge when price generates new swing highs and lows. Staying connected to these changes allows you to tailor your trading strategy to current market conditions.

Chapter 3

Anatomy of the Break and Retest Pattern

Parts of a Break and Retest Setup

A break and retest setup comprises of key factors that must be present for a high-probability trade. Throughout my years of trading forex, I've found four critical components. The first step is to construct a base, which is a firm support or resistance level that price has repeatedly obeyed. The strength of this level serves as the foundation for the overall setup. The breakout phase begins when the price moves forcefully through this level. Finally, the setup is completed with the retest phase, in which price returns to confirm the broken level.

Different Types of Breakouts

Throughout my trading experience, I've seen several different types of breakouts, each with its own set of characteristics. Clean breakouts occur when the price advances quickly through a level without hesitation. These generally result in the most dependable installations. Choppy breakouts exhibit more price oscillation near the breakout level, necessitating thorough study before trading. Explosive breakouts occur with sudden, tremendous momentum, usually during major news events or market openings.

The type of breakout determines your strategy to the subsequent retest. Trading EUR/USD taught me that clean breakouts usually provide the most straightforward retest opportunities. On my trading screen, I've seen price break cleanly through a level, then pull back for a retest before continuing in the breakout direction.

Characteristics of Valid Retest

A valid retest has unique qualities that distinguish it from a failed breakout. The retest should come with lower momentum than the initial break. Through several USD/JPY trades, I've seen that the most reliable retests show price gradually returning to the breached level, resulting in smaller candlesticks than during the breakout phase.

The depth of the retest is significant. Optimal retests return to the broken level without going too much beyond it. In my experience trading GBP/USD, retests that pierce slightly through the level frequently provide the finest entrances since they shake out weak positions before the big advance.

False Breakouts Versus True Breakouts

Distinguishing between fake and actual breakouts necessitates a thorough examination of several aspects. False breakouts usually have poor momentum during the break, followed by forceful advances back through the level. True breakouts have high initial momentum and remain above or below the broken level during the retest period.

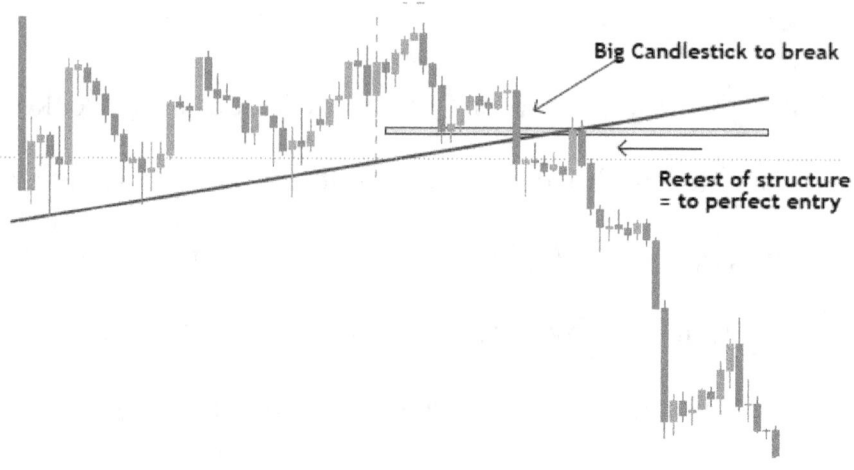

Volume is a critical factor in this differentiation. Years of market observation have shown me that actual break outs tend to occur with higher volume, but false breakouts frequently occur with lesser volume. This trend appears repeatedly across currency pairs and timeframes.

Reading Price Action During Retest

Price activity during the retest period provides key information regarding market intentions. When I trade retests on the AUD/USD, I look for specific candlestick shapes that indicate rejection of the tested level. Rejection candles, such as pins or engulfing patterns, provide important information regarding the probability that the trade will be successful.

The speed and character of price movement during retests provide valuable insights. Slow, grinding moves back to the level are frequently associated with a higher probability setup than abrupt, aggressive retests. This behaviour indicates that the market is cautiously testing the new support or resistance rather than outright rejecting it.

I've learnt through years of trading that understanding the intricacies of price action is critical for successful retest trading. Each retest has an own personality, shaped by market conditions, time of day, and the significance of the broken level.

The most dependable setups demonstrate clear price rejection at the retested level. Throughout my trading sessions, I've witnessed numerous examples of price approaching a level, forming a rejection candle, and then moving quickly in the breakout direction. These setups have the best risk-reward ratios and the highest probability of success.

In retest analysis, timing is also very important. Some retests appear immediately following the break, while others take days or even weeks to develop. This component is influenced by your trading timeframe and the significance of the broken level.

My experience has shown that higher timeframe retests frequently provide more solid trading opportunity.

A retest reinforces the setup by bringing together various technical factors. The probability of a successful trade increases dramatically when price movement corresponds with market structure, volume patterns, and overall trend direction. I've built my trading career on identifying and capitalising on these high-probability opportunities.

Understanding the anatomy of break and retest patterns requires time and experience. Each component contributes significantly to the overall success of the trade. You will develop the capacity to detect and trade these patterns by carefully studying these factors and acquiring experience through market observation.

Chapter 4

Entry and Exit Strategies

Optimal Entry Points During Retest

Finding a perfect entry point during a retest takes both expertise and patience. With my significant trading experience with the EUR/USD pair, I've created particular criteria for entry. The best entry point is when the price rebounds to the broken level and exhibits clear symptoms of rejection. You'll want to search for certain candlestick formations that indicate the retest has ended and the price is set to move on in the breakout direction.

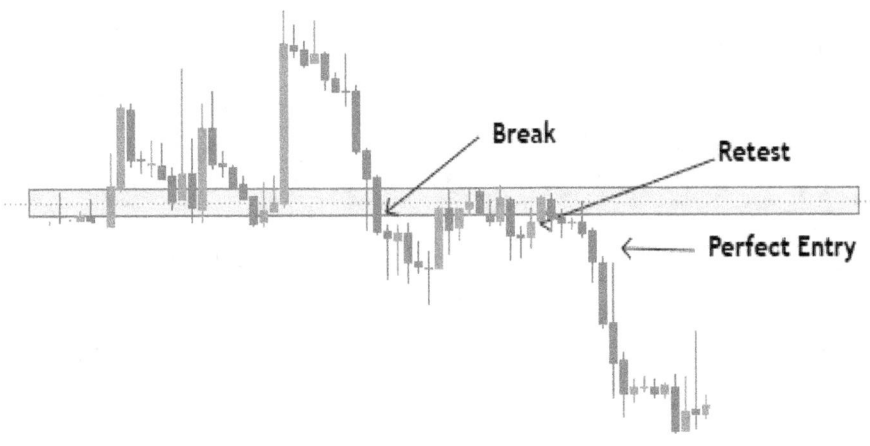

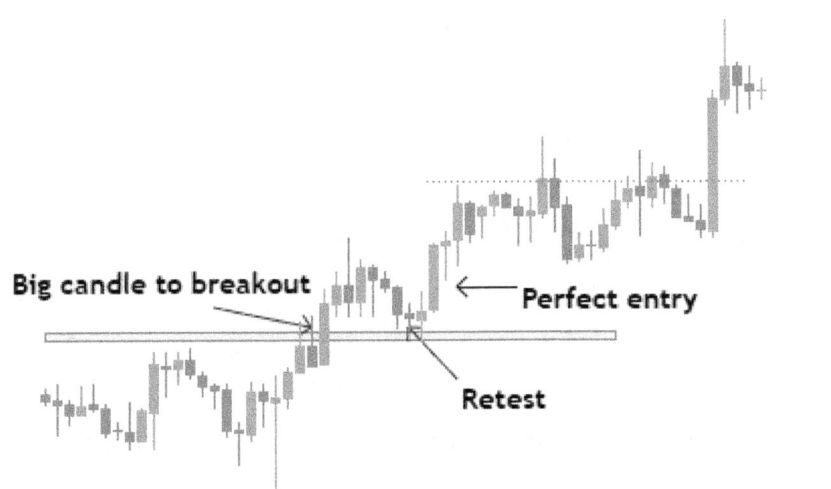

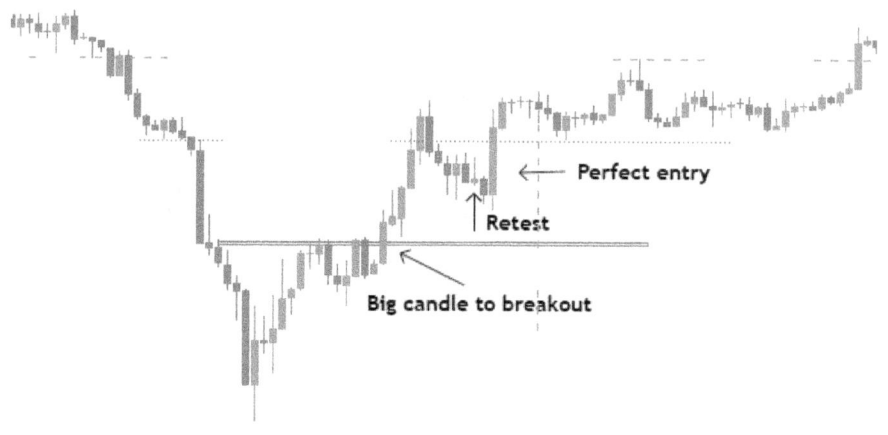

During my trading sessions, I frequently put limit orders just above the retested level. This approach captures the best rates while guaranteeing that the retest is legitimate. The goal is to determine the precise zone where previous support transforms into new resistance, or vice versa.

When trading GBP/USD, I've discovered that entering a few pips above the exact level typically results in higher fill prices and minimises the likelihood of being stopped out by normal market noise.

Stop Loss Placement Strategies

A break and retest trade is made or broken by the placement of its stop loss. After years of trading, I've honed my approach to stop placement depending on market structure. The most successful stop losses are located beyond the point where the break and retest setup becomes invalid. On the USD/JPY pair, this usually entails setting stops beyond the most recent swing high or low that precedes the breakout.

Your stop loss must allow the trade to breathe while keeping a reasonable risk-reward ratio. I've learnt from hard experience that tight stops frequently result in premature exits.

The market requires space to move naturally without hitting a stop during regular price swings.

Taking Profits: Multiple Target Approaches.

Profit-taking necessitates a smart approach. I use a multi-target method to maximise prospective gains while maintaining earnings along the way. The initial objective is frequently located near the preceding swing's high or low point in the breakout direction. Subsequent targets include higher-timeframe levels or major psychological pricing points.

Trading AUD/USD taught me the importance of scaling out of holdings. By taking partial profits at predefined levels, you can lock in gains while being open to possibly greater moves. This approach aids in the psychological aspects of trading, as securing a profit lessens the emotional stress of holding the entire position.

Position Size and Risk Management

Position sizing is the foundation of professional trading. In my approach, I risk a predetermined proportion of my trading money on each setup, usually 1-2%. This standardised approach assures that no single trade can have a substantial impact on your account, even during losing streaks. When trading NZD/USD, I compute position sizes based on the distance from my stop loss, ensuring that risk is consistent throughout trades.

The relationship between position size and market volatility requires attention. During high-impact news events or volatile market conditions, I frequently cut position sizes to account for larger stops and higher market uncertainty. This adaptable approach has helped me protect my capital during difficult market conditions.

Trading Psychology for Live Trades

Traders frequently struggle with the psychological aspects of managing live trades. Over the years of trading, I've developed tactics for maintaining emotional balance. One important approach is to have a clear trading strategy in place before starting each position. This strategy comprises planned entry points, stop losses, and profit targets, which minimises the impact of emotional decision-making throughout the trade.

During my CAD/JPY trades, I noticed how emotions can influence trading decisions. Fear may drive you to exit lucrative trades too early, whilst greed may lead you holding losing positions for too long. The key is to strictly adhere to your specified trading plan.

When handling winning trades, it is critical to consider the psychology of break and retest trading. As profits rise, the desire to depart early grows. I've learnt to trust my analysis and let profitable trades run to their targets, even when my emotions say otherwise.

Managing losing trades requires equal psychological discipline. Early in my trading career, I frequently increased stops or added to failing positions, expecting that the market would recover. Experience has taught me the importance of accepting small losses fast when trades go against my analysis.

The most effective traders are emotionally detached from individual trade outcomes. With years of market experience, I've learnt to see each trade as part of a broader statistical sample rather than an emotional event. This perspective promotes consistency in execution and decision-making.

Break and retest trading success is mainly reliant on your ability to execute your method consistently. Each entry, stop loss, and profit goal selection should be consistent with your entire trading strategy. The market will test your willpower, but staying disciplined during difficult times leads to long-term success.

Your trading mindset has a direct impact on your ability to identify and execute profitable entrances and exits. Maintaining emotional equilibrium allows you to observe market situations clearly and make sound judgements based on analysis rather than fear or greed.

Chapter 5

Break and retest under different market conditions.

Trading in Trending Markets

Trading break and retest patterns in trending markets provides some of the most reliable setups. During strong trends, breaks tend to follow the trend's direction, creating cleaner and more consistent trading opportunities. My experience trading EUR/USD has taught me that trending markets produce a series of breaks and retests as price moves in a specific direction.

In an uptrend, each break of resistance followed by a successful retest establishes a new support level. I've discovered that these retests frequently provide good entry points for trend continuation trades. The goal is to recognise the strength of the trend before entering the trade. Strong trends have obvious higher highs and higher lows, making break and retest patterns more dependable.

Break and Retest in Range-Bounded Markets.

Range-bound markets offer distinct problems and opportunities for break and retest traders. After countless hours of trading USD/JPY, I've discovered that ranges provide well-defined levels for possible breakouts. The main difference in range markets is the higher risk of false breaks, which necessitates more thorough validation before making trades.

You'll notice that ranges frequently generate many tests for both support and resistance levels. These repeated testing reinforce the levels, making future breaks more important. However, trading these breaks requires extra confirmation because prices frequently revert to the range following false breakouts.

Adapting to Different Market Sessions.

Each major forex trading session has distinct elements that influence break and retest patterns. The Asian session often exhibits more ranging behaviour, but the London and New York sessions frequently create bigger trending moves. Through years of trading GBP/USD, I've seen how these session factors affect breakthrough success rates.

Breaks tend to be less dependable during the Asian session due to lesser volume and volatility. The London open frequently results in higher volatility, which presents both opportunities and risks for break and retest traders. My trading strategy reflects these session-specific traits, altering position sizes and profit targets accordingly.

Impact of Market Volatility

Market volatility has a substantial impact on break-and-retest trading success. High volatility can produce dramatic breaks, but it can also result in whipsaw price movement during retests. Trading AUD/USD in tumultuous markets taught me how to change my entry and exit points dependent on market conditions.

During extremely volatile periods, stops require extra space to account for higher price fluctuations. I've learnt to minimise position sizes at these occasions in order to maintain consistent risk levels despite broader stops. Profit targets may also need to be adjusted, as volatile markets can cause bigger movements in shorter durations.

Trading multiple currency pairs.

Understanding the unique characteristics of each currency pair is required when applying break and retest tactics.

Some pairs, such as EUR/USD, exhibit cleaner breaks and retests due to their strong liquidity. Others, such as GBP/JPY, frequently exhibit more volatile price action, necessitating various strategy changes.

Recognising these differences and modifying your strategy to them is critical to your success when trading several pairs. With years of trading experience, I've discovered that each currency pair has its own personality. Some people respond better to specific types of breaks than others.

The correlation between currency pairings influences break and retest trading. When trading correlated pairs, similar patterns frequently appear concurrently. I've discovered that these connections can help validate trade setups, especially when numerous pairs exhibit large breaks.

The issue in trading many pairs is staying focused and avoiding overtrading. My strategy entails looking for setups across key pairings while ensuring that each trade fulfils specific criteria. This selected method promotes trading discipline while maximising opportunities.

High-impact news events have distinct effects on different currency pairs. Major economic releases can result in strong breaks and retests, but they also raise the possibility of false breaks. Your strategy must take into account these events and their potential influence on various currency pairs.

Success in changing market conditions necessitates flexibility and adaptability. I've learnt throughout the years of trading different pairings in different market conditions that no single strategy is always effective. The goal is to recognise current market conditions and alter your trading parameters accordingly.

Aligning your strategy with current market conditions might lead to the most profitable break and retest trades. Understanding how market conditions affect price action helps your trading performance, whether you're trading trends, ranges, or transitions between them.

Chapter 6

Advanced Break and Retest Concepts

Complex Break and Retest Patterns

Trading complex break and retest patterns demands much knowledge and experience. During my years of trading EUR/USD, I've seen several versions of these patterns. Double breaks happen when the price breaks a level, retests it, and then breaks it again before the last retest. These setups frequently result in greater moves due to increased market participation at each break point.

Hidden retests occur when the price does not return immediately to the broken level, but instead forms a new structure that serves as a retest. I learnt to spot these subtle patterns while trading USD/JPY. They frequently arise on longer timeframes and, once identified, can result in powerful moves.

Multiple Timeframe Analysis

Using multiple timeframe analysis substantially improves break and retest trading. I begin with larger timeframes to identify important levels and trend direction, then move to smaller timeframes to determine precise entry times. This method provides a full perspective of market structure and enhances trade timing.

The relationship between timeframes generates unique trading opportunities. A break on a lower timeframe may indicate a retest on a higher timeframe. During my

GBP/USD trades, I've found that synchronising break and retest signals over various timeframes boosts the likelihood of a successful trade.

Combining with Other Technical Indicators.

While price action remains the key driver, several technical indicators help in break and retest trading. Moving averages frequently provide dynamic support and resistance levels to supplement static break and retest points. I've carefully integrated these tools to ensure that they support, rather than replace, price action analysis.

Momentum indicators help to validate breaks and retests. I've found through years of trading experience that divergence between price and momentum during retests frequently indicates possible trade opportunity. These signals are especially potent when combined with a strong market structure.

Advanced Price Action Signals

Subtle price movement cues frequently precede major breaks and retests. Compression patterns, in which price action gets progressively tight prior to a break, typically result in large moves. My experience trading AUD/USD has proven that these compression patterns, when combined with break and retest setups, result in high-probability trades.

The nature of price activity during retests provides important information. Strong retests demonstrate a clear rejection of the broken level, frequently generating distinctive candlestick patterns. I pay close attention to the size and positioning of candle wicks because they convey valuable information about buying and selling pressure.

Market Manipulation Awareness

Understanding market manipulation strategies leads to better break and retest trading performance. Before the major move occurs, large market participants frequently place stops above resistance or below support. I've learnt to recognise these manipulation patterns and change my trading strategy accordingly by trading NZD/USD.

Stop hunts are typically seen around key break and retest levels. These actions shake out weak positions before the market swings in the desired direction. Recognising these patterns helps to prevent hasty exits and enhances trade timing.

The confluence of retail and institutional order flows results in predictable patterns. Major banks and financial institutions frequently place huge orders at important levels, resulting in zones where breaks and retests are more likely. Understanding this relationship leads to better trade selection and risk management.

Advanced break and retest trading necessitates patience and discipline. False signals are especially often near key levels, as large players try to trap retail traders. My years of experience have taught me to wait for unambiguous confirmation before entering a trade.

The most profitable configurations frequently integrate several advanced principles. A break and retest pattern that is consistent with multiple timeframe analysis, has unambiguous price action indications, and occurs at an institutional order level indicates a high-probability trade opportunity.

Understanding market dynamics beyond simple price patterns is essential for successful advanced break and retest trading. The relationship between market players, the impact of order flow, and the influence of several timeframes all play a role in trading performance.

Recognising and adjusting to these advanced principles is critical to your success as a break and retest trader. Consistent practice and observation reveal these patterns, resulting in better trade selection and execution.

The incorporation of advanced concepts should improve, not complicate, your trading strategy. I've found that keeping things simple while adding these components produces the best results. Each advanced thought should have a distinct role in your trading strategy.

Chapter 7

Trading Psychology and Risk Management

Emotional Control during Breakouts

Trading psychology is critical to successful break-and-retest trading. Throughout my years of trading EUR/USD, I've learnt that regulating emotions during breakouts is critical to long-term success. The excitement of seeing a stock break through a significant level might lead to impulsive trading. You must maintain emotional balance by waiting for sufficient retest confirmation before entering trade.

Strong breakouts can cause FOMO (Fear Of Missing Out), which tempts traders to chase price. I've created specialised strategies to deal with these emotional impulses. Taking deep breaths, walking away from the screen for a bit, and revisiting my trading rules all help me remain objective during these important moments.

Managing Fear and Greed.

Fear and greed are the two main emotional hurdles in forex trading. When trading USD/JPY breakouts, fear may keep you from entering valid setups, but greed may lead to overleveraging or premature entrances. I've discovered that keeping a trading log helps me detect emotional tendencies and build tactics to combat them.

During retest phases, the dread of failure often becomes more intense. As price approaches the broken level, doubts arise about the setup's veracity.

Through experience, I've learnt to trust my analysis and stick to my trading strategy, regardless of my emotional reactions to market movements.

Position Sizing Strategies

Position sizing is the foundation of professional risk management. My strategy involves estimating position sizes depending on account equity and the distance from my stop loss. Trading GBP/USD showed me that constant position sizing, independent of previous trade outcomes, results in continuous account growth.

Your position size should never be affected by emotions or recent trading performance. I follow stringent risk-per-trade guidelines, often risking no more than 1-2% of my trading money on any single position. This methodical technique guards against emotional trading decisions and large drawdowns.

Risk-Reward Optimisation

Optimising risk-reward ratios has a substantial impact on trading success. I've learnt from trading AUD/USD that looking for setups with a risk-reward ratio of at least 1:2 increases long-term profitability. Each trade should provide a substantial potential benefit to warrant the risk taken.

The relationship between risk and return fluctuates according on market conditions. During trending markets, I typically want bigger reward multiples, whereas range markets may necessitate more conservative targets. Your capacity to adjust these ratios to current market conditions boosts trading performance.

Creating and Maintaining Trading Discipline

Trading discipline comes through the consistent application of rules and processes. When I trade NZD/USD, I follow a predetermined trading strategy. This comprises entry requirements, position sizing, stop placement, and profit taking. Consistently following these standards increases confidence and lowers emotional decision-making.

During instances of decline, your trading discipline is put to the ultimate test. I've been through difficult times in which maintaining discipline became critical for survival. Sticking to your trading principles during these periods is sometimes critical to your long-term performance in the forex market.

Consecutive losses test every trader's discipline. Years of trading experience have taught me that keeping consistent risk management even during losing streaks saves capital and mental sanity. Regardless of previous outcomes, each trade is treated equally in terms of analytical attention and risk management.

Mental preparation is essential for keeping trading discipline. Before each trading session, I go over my trading rules and the current market conditions. This exercise helps to build the correct mentality for making disciplined trading selections.

Break and retest trading needs both technical expertise and psychological strength. The ability to maintain emotional control while following your trading strategy consistently leads to better performance over time. Instead of being an emotive event, each trade is incorporated into a broader statistical sample.

Managing risk effectively necessitates ongoing monitoring and self-awareness. After years of trading various currency pairs, I've discovered that risk management protects both capital and psychology. A single overleveraged trade can erase months of diligent trading, causing long-term psychological damage.

The most successful traders adhere to strict risk management regardless of market conditions or recent performance. Your risk-taking strategy should be consistent regardless of whether you're on a winning or losing trend. This constancy provides the foundation for long-term trading success.

Chapter 8

Common Break and Retest Patterns

Horizontal Support/Resistance Breaks

Horizontal support and resistance breaks are the most common break and retest patterns. During my years of trading EUR/USD, I've found that these patterns are most accurate when the levels have been tested several times. The idea is to locate strong horizontal levels where prices have consistently reversed.

Trading these patterns demands a grasp of each level's power. You'll notice that horizontal levels get stronger with each successful test.

In my experience trading GBP/USD, the most winning setups occur when price breaks a well-established horizontal level and then returns for a precise retest.

Trendline Breaks and Retests

When properly detected, trendline breaks can provide tremendous trading opportunities. I've spent numerous hours analysing USD/JPY trendline breaks, and I discovered that the angle of the trendline has a significant impact on the reliability of the break and retest pattern. While moderately inclined trendlines often create cleaner retests, steeper trendlines frequently lead to more volatile breaks.

Your success in trading trendline breaks is dependent on correct trendline drawing. Through years of effort, I've learnt to connect significant swing highs and lows while ensuring that the trendline contacts at least three spots.

The most dependable breaks occur when the price advances firmly through a well-established trendline.

Chart Pattern Breakouts

Chart patterns arise as a result of price activity and present unique break and retest possibilities. Trading AUD/USD has taught me to recognise a variety of patterns, including triangles, wedges, and rectangles. Each pattern type produces various break and retest conditions, necessitating somewhat different trading strategies.

Chart patterns that are completed frequently lead to powerful directional moves. I've noticed that breaks from symmetrical triangles typically result in sharp moves, followed by obvious retests. Your ability to detect these patterns early on enhances trade timing and risk management.

Double bottom

Bullish Flag

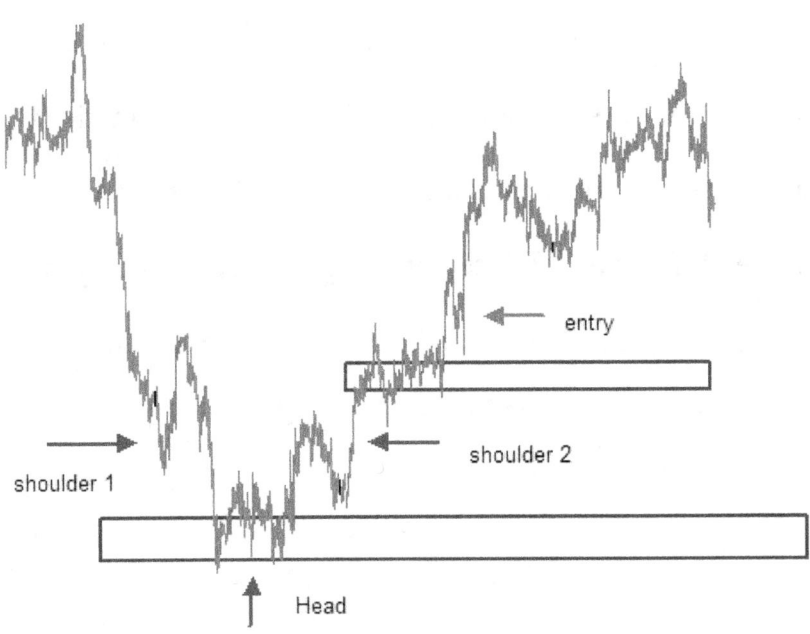

Moving Average Breaks

Moving average breaks give dynamic support and resistance levels for breakout and retest trading. The 200-period moving average has been found to be very significant in my trading of NZD/USD. Price frequently respects these dynamic levels, resulting in consistent break and retest possibilities.

Break and retest trading get more complex due to the interaction of several moving averages. When price breaks through clustered moving averages, the retest is typically more significant. These setups typically lead to persistent moves in the break out direction, according to my experience.

Channel Breakouts

Channel breakouts happen when price breaks through established trading channels. Trading CAD/JPY channel breaks has taught me that the width and duration of the channel affect the reliability of subsequent retests. Wider channels usually result in more significant swings following genuine breaks.

Your approach to channel breakouts should take into account the general market situation. Years of observation have taught me that breaks that occur in the direction of the greater trend are more likely to be successful. The retest of broken channel boundaries frequently yields outstanding entry opportunities.

The psychology that underpins these frequent patterns determines their reliability. Large market participants frequently exploit these well-known patterns to deceive retail traders. Understanding this dynamic helps to avoid false breaks and optimise trade timing.

Trading these patterns demands discipline and patience. Not every break results in a tradable retest, and not every retest leads to further movement. Through trading several currency pairs, I've learnt to wait for unambiguous confirmation before taking positions.

The interaction of various pattern types generates complex trading opportunities. A trendline break may coincide with the completion of a chart pattern, adding power to the whole setup. These pattern convergences frequently yield the most winning trade for me.

Proper risk management remains critical when trading frequent patterns. The popularity of these setups may lead to increased market manipulation at crucial levels. Your stop placement should account for natural market volatility while protecting against false breaks.

Understanding the unique qualities of these patterns is necessary for effective trading. Each pattern type has the ideal entry locations, stop levels, and profit targets. Recognising and trading these patterns becomes easier with repeated practice and observation.

The most dependable arrangements incorporate several pattern kinds. A horizontal level break coincides with a channel breakout and moving average support, indicating a high-probability trading opportunity. These confluences boost the opportunity of a successful trade.

Chapter 9

Real trading examples and case studies.

Successful Trade Analysis.

My most winning EUR/USD trade came during a huge trend reversal. The daily chart revealed a significant downturn that had lasted several weeks. Price established a clear support level at 1.0850, tested it several times, and then broke above with great impetus. The subsequent retest gave an ideal entrance opportunity. I entered at 1.0855 after noticing a heavy rejection candle at the retested level. The trade generated 120 pips as the price approached the next big resistance level.

You'll find similar opportunity across currency pairs. Analysing successful trades reveals patterns that can be duplicated. Strong level breaks, obvious retests, and good market context all support the trade direction.

Failed Trade Analysis

Learning from failed trades is as beneficial. Trading USD/JPY taught me this lesson when I entered a break and retest position that appeared fantastic on the 4-hour chart. However, I neglected to note the contradicting tendency on a daily basis. The trade soon went against my position, triggering my stop loss. This experience emphasised the importance of studying multiple timeframes.

Your trading experience will contain both successes and losses. By documenting bad trades, I've discovered frequent faults that lead to losses. These insights help to improve trading methods and future performance.

Market Context Examples

In break and retest trading, market context is key. During my GBP/USD trades, I've noticed how varied market conditions impact setup reliability. One especially interesting case occurred during a significant rise. Price broke over a crucial resistance level at 1.3200, although the retest occurred amid strong economic news. The extra volatility resulted in a deeper retest than usual, shaking out many traders before continuing upward.

The underlying market structure influences break and retest behaviour. I've learnt to determine which market conditions promote dependable breaks and which may lead to misleading moves by trading various scenarios.

Various Currency Pair Examples

During breaks and retests, each currency pair has its own distinct features.

Trading AUD/USD showed me how commodity-linked currencies frequently generate different retest patterns than major pairs. One notable trade featured the breakdown of a long-term trendline. The retest period lasted longer than usual in EUR/USD settings, necessitating additional patience before the eventual move.

Your strategy must adapt to the personalities of each couple. Through considerable market monitoring, I've devised unique criteria for several currency pairs. Some people respond better to specific patterns, whereas others require other entry and exit tactics.

Managing Unexpected Market Events

Unexpected circumstances put your risk management and trading approach to the test. During the 2015 Swiss Franc shock, I experienced how unexpected market movements can alter break and retest patterns.

This event provided critical lessons regarding position sizing and the importance of strict risk management, regardless of how comfortable you are with a setup.

The currency market frequently provides unforeseen obstacles. Through years of trading experience, I've learnt to prepare for a variety of scenarios by maintaining proper position sizes and explicit risk management procedures.

Market volatility can surge unexpectedly, harming current trades. My strategy includes lowering position sizes during potentially volatile periods and widening stops to allow for increased market movement. This adaptive method protects capital amid unexpected situations.

To be successful in break and retest trading, you must understand how different market scenarios effect trade outcomes. Patterns form from the analysis of different examples across multiple currency pairs, which guide future trading decisions.

Documenting both successful and unsuccessful trades offers significant learning opportunities. Your trading log should include a thorough examination of market conditions, entrance motivations, and outcome explanations. This record can help you find patterns in your trading outcomes.

Difficult market conditions frequently provide the most valuable learning opportunities. Through trading in various market circumstances, I've created tactics for adapting to shifting conditions while retaining constant risk management.

Real-world trading examples highlight the importance of patience and discipline. You'll notice that the finest setups frequently necessitate extended periods of price action before presenting clear entry points.

Experience and self-assurance are gained through the management of trades across a variety of market conditions. Each trading scenario expands your knowledge base, enhancing your future decision-making ability. Technical analysis, risk management, and market knowledge together lead to consistent trading outcomes.

Chapter 10

Creating Your Break and Retest Trading Plan

Creating A Trading Checklist

A comprehensive trading checklist serves as the cornerstone for successful break and retest trading. Through years of trading EUR/USD, I've honed my checklist to capture the key components of high-probability setups. Each item indicates an important factor that must be aligned before engaging in a trade.

My trading checklist begins with a market structure analysis. You'll need to identify the main trend direction, critical support and resistance levels, and any notable chart patterns. The strength of possible trading levels is evaluated using a variety of criteria, including the amount of touches and the time frame in which they emerge.

Developing Entry Rules

The entry rules must be specific and objective. Trading the USD/JPY has taught me the importance of having defined entry criteria to avoid making emotional decisions. The first criteria focusses on the break itself: price must move decisively through the level, with great velocity and volume.

Your entry rules should contain requirements for the retest phase. From my trading expertise, I've learnt that valid retests often exhibit declining momentum as the price approaches the broken level. The emergence of rejection candles at these levels frequently presents excellent entry points.

Establishing exit criteria

Exit requirements deserve the same care as entry rules. When trading GBP/USD, I set numerous profit targets dependent on the market structure. The initial objective is frequently at the next important level, while subsequent targets expand to longer-term resistance or support zones.

Stop loss placement adheres to particular rules based on market structure. Stops must be placed beyond the point at which the break and retest scenario becomes invalid, according to my years of trading. This approach protects against normal market swings while keeping risk levels moderate.

Risk Management Guidelines

Professional trading is based on risk management principles. I've developed tight parameters for trading AUD/USD, limiting risk per trade to 1-2% of total trading capital. This cautious approach assures survival in difficult market conditions and promotes long-term success.

Position sizing calculations must take into account the present market volatility. Your risk each trade remains constant, but position size varies according to stop loss distance. This dynamic approach ensures consistent risk levels across a variety of trading scenarios.

Performance Tracking and Analysis

Performance tracking gives valuable feedback for strategy refinement. My trading log has complete information for each trade, including setup quality, market conditions, and outcome analysis. This paperwork assists in identifying patterns in both successful and failed trades.

Track specified metrics to assess strategy efficacy. You'll be able to identify which setups perform better under different market conditions by systematically recording trade data. This analysis informs future trading decisions and helps you fine-tune your approach.

A comprehensive review of trading results shows opportunities for improvement. I analyse my trading journal on a regular basis to identify patterns in my decision-making. This analysis frequently reveals small changes that can enhance overall performance.

Regular strategy assessments keep your trading plan up to date. Your trading approach must adjust as the markets change. Your trading plan will stay effective in the face of shifting market conditions if it is constantly evaluated and refined.

Documentation is extremely important in strategy formulation. Every facet of your approach, from initial market analysis to trade management and exit strategies, should be detailed in your trading plan. This detailed paper outlines clear principles for live trading.

Success in break and retest trading necessitates adherence to your trading plan. Through years of market experience, I've learnt that consistency in execution is more important than individual trade outcomes. Following your plan helps you stay disciplined amid difficult market conditions.

Creating a trading plan takes time and experience. Each trade offers insights that can help you improve your approach. The combination of clear rules, good risk management, and systematic analysis forms a solid foundation for persistent trading performance.

While keeping key principles, your trading plan should adapt based on market experience. You'll identify which components of your strategy function best in various market scenarios through rigorous recording and analysis. This understanding leads to continual improvements in trading performance.

Chapter 11

Advanced Strategy Optimisation.

Fine-Tuning Entry Points

Tailoring entry points necessitates a thorough understanding of price action and market behaviour. I've learnt minor signs that increase entry timing by trading EUR/USD. The way price approaches a retested level frequently provides signals about probable trade results. Small rejection candles formed at precise retest levels usually yield better entries than larger candles formed away from the level.

Your entry refinement process should be centred on price action details. I've learnt to recognise distinct candlestick forms that imply higher probability trades after years of studying USD/JPY price movement. The relationship between candle bodies and wicks during retests reveals important information regarding market mood.

Optimising Stop Loss Placement

Stop loss optimisation strikes a compromise between preventing false breaks and allowing trades to grow. When trading GBP/USD, I set my stops beyond major structure points rather than utilising predetermined pip distances. This method adjusts for each pair's distinct volatility characteristics while maintaining optimal risk management.

The optimisation of stop placement entails analysing price movements around important levels. Through considerable market monitoring, I have discovered typical retracement depths during genuine retests. This understanding allows you to place stops at levels that safeguard against regular market noise while preventing premature departures.

Maximising Profit Targets

To set optimal profit targets, you must first comprehend market structure and price behaviour. Trading AUD/USD taught me how to identify high-probability target zones using historical support and resistance levels. The most reliable targets frequently coincide with numerous technical criteria, such as swing points and psychological price levels.

Your profit-taking strategy should adapt to the current market conditions. Through trading in numerous market settings, I've learnt to change target distances based on volatility and trend strength. Strong trends frequently enable broader targets, whereas range markets necessitate more conservative profit goals.

Adapting to Market Change

Successful traders distinguish themselves from the competition through their ability to adapt to market conditions. During my NZD/USD trades, I've seen how market behaviour changes with time. Strategies that were effective in prior months may need to be adjusted if volatility patterns change.

The ability to identify changing market conditions is critical for strategy optimisation.

You'll be able to recognise trends in market behaviour that necessitate strategic modifications by carefully monitoring price action and market structure. These modifications may have an impact on entry timing, stop placement, and profit targets.

Strategy Evolution and Refinement

Strategy refinement is accomplished through rigorous study of trading performance. My strategy is a regular evaluation of completed trades to identify trends in both successful and unsuccessful setups. This study identifies potential areas for improvement while adhering to the strategy's key concepts.

The evolution of your trading strategy should maintain effective features while strengthening poor ones.

Through my trading expertise, I've discovered that simple modifications frequently result in huge improvements in total performance. These modifications may include entry requirements, risk management regulations, or trade management procedures.

Advanced optimisation necessitates an awareness of the relationships between various strategy components. The combination of entry timing, stop placement, and profit targets determines your strategy's overall risk-reward profile. Through rigorous investigation, you will discover ideal combinations that improve trading performance.

Maintaining detailed trading records is critical to successful strategy optimisation. Your trading log should include particular details about each trade, such as entry quality, market conditions, and outcome analysis. This documentation lays the groundwork for major strategy enhancements.

Analysing lost trades is frequently the most effective way to improve strategy. Through a rigorous review of failed setups, I discovered tiny trends that will help me avoid similar losses in future trades. This approach increases strategy robustness while boosting overall performance.

Strategy optimisation necessitates patience and systematic testing. Through a rigorous examination of trading records, you will discover which tweaks yield regular profits. The goal is to improve strategy effectiveness while retaining risk management standards.

The refinement process never fully ends with trading. Markets continually change, necessitating continuing strategy adaption. Your strategy must be adaptable while keeping key concepts that produce consistent results.

Trading success stems from ongoing development and adaption. I've learnt from years of market experience that strategy optimisation is a process, not a destination.

Each market cycle brings new insights into prospective strategy enhancements.

Chapter 12

Common Mistakes and How to Avoid them

Early Entry Mistakes

Early entries are among the most common mistakes in break and retest trading. Through EUR/USD trading, I've seen countless traders enter trades without adequate confirmation. The exhilaration of watching price approach a broken level frequently leads to early entries. You must fight this desire and wait for clear rejection signals on retested levels.

During big market movements, the desire to enter early becomes more intense.

Trading USD/JPY taught me that patience during retest periods pays off handsomely. Instead of chasing prices, skilled traders await particular confirmation patterns before committing to positions.

Stop Loss Errors

Stop loss mistakes can have disastrous consequences for trading accounts. During my years of trading GBP/USD, I've noticed three major stop loss errors. The first is establishing stops too tightly, leading to premature exits during regular market volatility. Second, instead of market structure, stop placement is based on random pip distances. Third, moving stops to breakeven too rapidly, which frequently results in missed opportunity.

Your stop loss placement must be based on market structure and volatility. I've learnt from considerable market observation that stops require breathing room while keeping reasonable risk levels. The objective is to place stops beyond the positions that would invalidate the trading arrangement.

Position Sizing Issues.

Emotional trading decisions can lead to position sizing mistakes. When trading the AUD/USD, I've seen traders raise their position sizes after losses in the hopes of recovering swiftly. This unsafe technique tends to lead to higher losses and psychological stress.

The ideal strategy includes regular position sizing based on account equity and stop distance. I've maintained rigorous guidelines that restrict risk every trade over my years of trading experience. This systematic approach protects capital amid drawdowns and promotes long-term profitability.

Psychology-Based Mistakes

Trading psychology effects all aspects of break and retest trading. Fear and greed are common mistakes that jeopardise trading performance. I've learnt how emotions may trump rational decision-making through trading NZD/USD, leading to poor trade execution.

Your emotional state influences trade selection and management. Through my market experience, I've found particular psychological patterns that lead to mistakes. FOMO motivates early entry, fear prompts premature withdrawal, and greed leads to overleveraging. Recognising these trends aids in maintaining trading discipline.

Strategy Implementation Errors

During live trading, it's common to make implementation mistakes. When trading CAD/JPY, I have seen traders deviate from their trading strategy due to market pressure. This discrepancy reduces strategy efficacy and causes avoidable losses.

The solution requires strict adherence to specified trading rules. You can avoid common strategy errors by putting a systematic trading plan into place. Each trade should adhere to particular criteria for entry, stop placement, and profit targets.

Common implementation errors include neglecting market context, trading against key trends, and failing to respond to changing market conditions. My trading experience demonstrates that effective implementation necessitates both discipline and flexibility.

Technical analysis mistakes are common among break and retest traders. I've learnt over years of chart research to avoid common trade errors such as pressing trades on weak levels or ignoring various timeframe analysis. These mistakes frequently lead to poor trade choices and unintended losses.

To succeed in break and retest trading, avoid these common errors. You can dramatically improve your trading outcomes by paying close attention to entry timing, effective stop placement, consistent position sizing, and emotional control.

Risk management mistakes frequently exacerbate other trading errors. I've seen how poor risk management exacerbates the impact of technical or psychological mistakes while trading various currency pairings. Maintaining rigorous risk management helps to mitigate the damage caused by inevitable trading errors.

Identifying and correcting trading mistakes leads to greater performance. Specific mistakes and their impact on results should be documented in your trading log. This study helps to prevent similar errors in future trades while also boosting the overall trading strategy.

Learning from mistakes speeds up trading development. You will discover trends that deserve attention by conducting a systematic examination of trading errors. This practice improves trading skills while instilling confidence in your approach.

Conclusion

Your Journey in Break and Retest Trading

Break and retest trading is an effective approach to forex market analysis and trading. Throughout my fifteen years of trading expertise, I've seen how this strategy has helped struggling traders become consistent performers. The journey to mastering break and retest trading needs effort, patience, and ongoing education.

Understanding market structure is the first step towards successful break and retest trading. The way prices interact with important levels reveals information about market participants' intentions. Through careful observation and analysis, you'll learn to read these stories in real time and uncover high-probability trading opportunities.

Trading psychology is critical to your development. I've discovered that emotional control during breakouts and retests is often the determining factor in trading success. The ability to wait for suitable opportunities, maintain position sizing discipline, and stick to your trading plan throughout difficult periods lays the groundwork for consistent profits.

Risk management is the cornerstone of professional trading. Years of market experience have taught me that adequate risk management protects both trading capital and psychology. Each trade should risk a tiny, predefined percentage of your account to ensure survival during unavoidable drawdowns.

The technical features of break and retest trading require serious consideration. Understanding various breakout kinds, recognising genuine retests, and determining optimal entrance points requires practice and observation.

Your success depends on honing these talents while adhering to strict risk management rules.

Market conditions always change, necessitating strategy modification. I've learnt the value of flexibility via trading different currency pairings in different market circumstances. Your approach must adapt to shifting market conditions while adhering to fundamental trading concepts.

Trading success stems from avoiding frequent blunders. Early entrances, improper stop placement, and position sizing faults can all jeopardise even the greatest strategy. You will increase your opportunity of long-term success by being aware of these risks and committing to proper trading techniques.

The journey of mastering break and retest trading is never fully over. Markets develop, resulting in new difficulties and possibilities.

Your trading approach should be adaptable while keeping the focused execution that delivers consistent returns.

The strength of break and retest market is its ability to be used to a wide range of markets and periods. The ideas stay consistent whether you trade the 15-minute chart or the daily period. I've successfully utilised these approaches to key currency pairs, identifying reliable setups in a variety of market circumstances.

Your trading progress involves ongoing skill refinement. You can find trends that contribute to successful outcomes by observing market behaviour, analysing previous trades, and keeping careful records. Over time, this continual development process strengthens your trading approach.

Every trader's determination is put to the test by the psychological difficulties of break and retest trading. Fear during retests, greed during strong movements, and doubt during drawdowns call into question your dedication to correct trading techniques. You will overcome these problems by gaining strong emotional control and adhering to tight risk management guidelines.

Technical analysis abilities alone are insufficient for success in forex trading. A holistic trading approach is created by combining market knowledge, psychological discipline, and risk management. Each factor is critical to long-term trading success.

Regularly reviewing and assessing your trading performance offers opportunities for improvement. Analysing both successful and losing trades will help you uncover patterns in your trading behaviour. This analysis guides strategy refinement while preserving effective aspects of your approach.

Your trading journey will include both successes and setbacks. You will be able to endure difficult times and thrive during favourable market conditions if you practise appropriate risk management. Each encounter enhances your trading knowledge and skill growth.

The principles provided in this tutorial serve as a basis for successful trading. Through systematic application and continual learning, you will gain the skills required for consistent performance. Take these lessons and apply them with patience and discipline as you continue your trading journey.

Remember that success in break and retest trading requires consistent use of proven methods. Technical analysis, psychological discipline, and adequate risk management combine to provide a strong trading approach capable of producing consistent profits over a wide range of market situations.

Video Access Page

Thank you for purchasing my book! As a token of my appreciation, I've made available exclusive video content just for you.

To access your complimentary videos, simply visit:

https://mega.nz/folder/IYZRQZTL#UIoA3WK6Gb_OfS2Xxq-iRA

Thank you for your support, and I hope these additional resources enhance your reading experience!

Best regards,

James willy

www.ingramcontent.com/pod-product-compliance
Lightning Source LLC
Chambersburg PA
CBHW071035240526
45469CB00006BD/2213